False!

Popular Myths Debunked

by

Gia Accardi

SCHOLASTIC INC.
New York Toronto London Auckland
Sydney New Delhi Hong Kong

Illustrations by

Jason Raish

Copyright © 2012 by Scholastic Inc.
All rights reserved. Published by Scholastic Inc.
Printed in the U.S.A.

ISBN-13: 978-0-545-34069-4
ISBN-10: 0-545-34069-1
(meets NASTA specifications)

10 11 12 13   113   20 19 18 17 16

Contents

Introduction

Have you heard the saying "An apple a day keeps the doctor away"? Do you believe that bats are blind? Has anyone ever told you that elephants are afraid of mice? We hear ideas like these so often that it's easy to assume they are true. But in fact, many beliefs like these are just myths and rumors. In other words, they are ideas

that many believe to be true—but they are actually false.

On the following pages you will discover the truth about some popular myths and rumors. Some of these stories contain a little bit of truth. Others are totally false. All of them show how people attempt to understand the world.

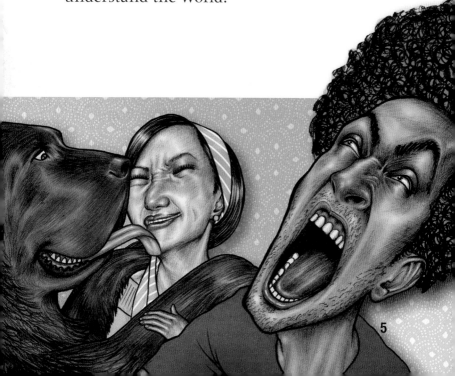

People love to give advice about food and health. But can you trust it?

CHAPTER

1 | Health Check

 IT'S SAFE TO EAT FOOD OFF THE GROUND IF IT'S BEEN THERE LESS THAN FIVE SECONDS.

Oops! You dropped your snack. That's okay. The "five-second rule" says the snack is safe to eat. Just pick it up within five seconds. That will keep it germ-free. Right?

A science student named Jillian Clarke decided to find out. She coated floor tiles with **bacteria**—germs. Then, she dropped food on the floor. She picked it up less than five seconds later. Next, she looked at it under a microscope. Guess what? Bacteria were all over the food!

It is tough to throw out a tasty snack. But a dropped snack might make you sick!

If your food falls on the ground, throw it out!

MYTH SOME SNACK CAKES STAY FRESH FOR 50 YEARS.

In the 1960s, many Americans feared a nuclear war. Some people even built shelters underground. They stocked the shelters with food. They chose items that would last a long time. A certain brand of snack cakes was a popular choice. People believed the cakes stayed fresh for 50 years.

Luckily, the U.S. did not face a nuclear war. So the snack cakes were never put to the test. That was lucky, too. In reality, these cakes spoil in only 25 days!

That is much sooner than 50 years! Still, it is a long time for baked goods to stay fresh. How do they last that long?

Homemade baked goods often contain dairy products, like milk and butter. Dairy spoils quickly. But the packaged cakes don't contain real dairy. So they stay fresh longer. Just don't eat that one you found in your kindergarten lunch box!

MYTH AN APPLE A DAY KEEPS THE DOCTOR AWAY.

Do you hate to go to the doctor? Just eat an apple every day. Rumor has it that apples keep you healthy. They "keep the doctor away." But is this rumor true?

Apples *are* good for you. They contain vitamin C. It can help keep you from catching colds. Apples also have many **nutrients**, which give you energy. But apples alone won't cure illness.

What would happen if you ate a variety of fruits? That would be better for you than eating only apples. Other fruits cannot cure illness, either. But studies show that eating different fruits can **improve** your health.

So, why is the myth only about apples? Maybe that is because apples are easy to grow. Maybe it is because apples stay fresh a long time. Or, maybe it's because "a melon a day keeps the doctor away" doesn't sound so good!

MYTH EATING CARROTS WILL GIVE YOU PERFECT EYESIGHT.

"Finish your carrots, or you will need glasses." Since the 1940s, this advice has been heard around many dinner tables. It might be an **effective** way to get kids to eat carrots. But is there any truth to it?

Well, carrots *are* a good source of vitamin A. And vitamin A has been connected to eye health. Without vitamin A, you might develop cataracts. A cataract happens when a part of your eye called the lens gets cloudy. That makes it hard to see.

Vitamin A can help prevent cataracts. But vitamin A—and carrots—will not give you perfect vision. So, how did this myth get started?

During World War II, the British fought the Germans. The British air force used secret radar. It let them spot German warplanes at night. The British didn't want the Germans to know about this radar. So, they spread a made-up story.

The British said their pilots ate lots of carrots. The carrots gave the pilots great night vision. Everyone believed the story. And the myth about carrots and eyesight took off.

Eating carrots did not give British pilots super vision.

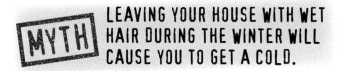

LEAVING YOUR HOUSE WITH WET HAIR DURING THE WINTER WILL CAUSE YOU TO GET A COLD.

You are late for school. You take a quick shower. Then, you run out the door. "Wait!" your mother yells. "Dry your hair. It's winter! You'll catch a cold!"

Guess what? Mom isn't always right. Going out with wet hair might not be a great idea. Your hair could freeze! But you cannot catch a cold from going out with wet hair in winter. There is only one way to catch a cold. You must be around someone who is **infected** with a cold **virus**.

How did the hair myth start? Maybe it's because people tend to catch colds in winter. Still, wet hair is not to blame. In winter, people spend lots of time indoors. Cold viruses spread easily from one person to another. And dry winter air causes the **mucus** in your nose to dry up. Without mucus to trap them, viruses get in. Yuck!

MYTH EATING TURKEY MAKES YOU SLEEPY.

It's Thanksgiving. You just finished eating dinner. Now, you feel very sleepy. That is no surprise. Everyone knows that turkey makes you sleepy. Right? Wrong!

Turkey contains a chemical called tryptophan. Tryptophan can make you sleepy. If you swallowed a big dose of it by itself, it would make you drowsy.

But what goes on when you eat turkey? You are not eating tryptophan by itself. You are eating it in turkey. And turkey is also full of protein. That gives you energy.

So, why do you feel sleepy after Thanksgiving dinner? It is not because of the turkey alone. It is because you ate so much other food.

Your body has to work overtime to **digest** a big meal. Breaking down all that food is tiring work!

Life can be dangerous—but maybe not as dangerous as you think.

CHAPTER 2 | Death and Disaster

MYTH A PENNY DROPPED FROM THE TOP OF A BIG SKYSCRAPER COULD KILL SOMEONE!

Are you worried about small change falling from tall buildings? Don't be!

Pennies are not built for speed. They are light. They are flat. What would happen if you dropped one off the Empire State Building? As it fell, the wind would toss it around. That would slow the penny down. If it hit someone, the penny might sting. But it would not kill the person!

In fact, the penny probably would not hit anyone. A gust of wind would just carry it away.

It is not likely that you will get hit by a high-speed penny.

15

MYTH EATING RICE CAUSES BIRDS TO EXPLODE.

What happens right after a wedding? You throw rice at the newly married couple. That may sound weird. But it is a tradition. It goes back to ancient times. Thousands of years ago, rice was a symbol of health and wealth.

But in recent years, many people have stopped throwing rice. Instead, they throw flower petals or birdseed. Why? A rumor spread. It said rice kills birds. They eat it after a wedding. It expands in their stomachs. Sometimes, the birds explode!

Luckily, this myth is not true. Wild birds eat rice from rice fields. And they don't explode. Scientists who study birds have said so. The USA Rice Federation has, too. They all agree that rice is good for birds.

Still, some people use flower petals instead. They look prettier. Plus, they are much easier to sweep up!

SITTING NEAR AN EXIT DURING AN AIRPLANE FLIGHT WILL INCREASE YOUR CHANCES OF SURVIVING A CRASH.

You are going on an airplane trip. You feel a little nervous. You hope to sit in an exit-row seat. You have heard these seats are safest in a plane crash.

Hold on! That is just a myth. Some magazine writers did a study. They researched every big jet accident from 1971 to 2005. They looked at all the **data.** They found that exit-row seats are not the safest. The safest seats are at the back of the plane.

Why? In a crash, the back is least likely to get crushed on **impact**. And it's far from the wings, which hold **flammable** jet fuel. So, the back is not as likely to catch fire.

However, airplanes rarely crash. Air travel is very safe. Your chance of dying in a crash is about one in 11 million! So sit where you like. Enjoy your trip!

MYTH A CHICKEN CAN SURVIVE WITHOUT ITS HEAD.

It sounds like a horror movie. A chicken gets its head chopped off. Yet, it keeps on running around! Is it a zombie chicken? Well, no, not exactly.

It is true that a headless chicken can run around the chicken yard! But that does not mean the chicken is still alive. So, what is really happening? The chicken's body does not realize that it is dead. *Huh?!*

Here is how it works. Like humans, every chicken has a brain stem down at the bottom of its brain. The brain stem controls reflexes. Those are the movements that your body makes automatically.

A chicken's head gets chopped off. But the brain stem is still attached to the chicken's body. It signals the chicken's muscles to move. For a few minutes, the chicken runs around. It looks alive. But it is dead. Yuck!

MYTH IT'S DANGEROUS TO SWIM AFTER EATING.

Has anyone ever told you this? "You just ate. So you cannot go swimming for one hour. If you do, you might get stomach cramps and drown."

Every year, millions of kids lose valuable swimming time. Why? Their parents believe this myth!

You can get cramps when your muscles are tired. You can get cramps when your diet lacks salt. Sometimes, diseases cause cramps. But most experts agree that eating does not cause cramps—not even if you swim right after you eat.

So how did this myth get started? No one is sure. But picture this. A family is on a picnic. The kids want to swim after lunch. The parents just want to relax. They don't want to watch the kids swim. So they tell the kids they must wait for one hour. Maybe that is how this myth began!

Famous people have had some truly odd rumors spread about them.

CHAPTER
3
The Rich and Famous

WALT DISNEY HAD HIS BODY FROZEN AFTER HE DIED.

Have you heard of Walt Disney? He is the guy who created Mickey Mouse. In 1966, Disney died from lung cancer. His funeral was small. Not many people **witnessed** his burial. Soon, a weird rumor started.

People said Disney did not really die. Instead, he had his body frozen. He would be thawed out when doctors found a cure for cancer.

Many people believed the story. The freezing idea was big at the time. And Disney seemed bold—and rich—enough to try it. Alas, in truth, he really did die.

In spite of popular belief,
Walt Disney is not chilling
in a block of ice.

21

MYTH QUEEN MARIE ANTOINETTE SAID, "LET THEM EAT CAKE!"

In the late 1700s, the people of France were poor. They had to pay high taxes to support the king and queen. And they were not happy about it.

Marie Antoinette was the queen of France. She was rich and spoiled. And she did not seem to care about anybody else.

Marie became **infamous** for a clueless remark. Someone told her that the people had no bread to eat. They could not afford it. Marie said they should eat cake instead!

This reply was very **offensive.** It showed how little she cared about starving people. But did Marie really say it?

The story was written in a book. The book was published in 1767. That was years before Marie became queen. Experts say another French queen made the remark. Marie may have been clueless. But maybe she wasn't as bad as people think!

MYTH GEORGE WASHINGTON HAD WOODEN TEETH.

Can you imagine getting a splinter in your tongue? Ouch!

Well, it might have happened to the first American president. It might have, anyway, if a certain myth were true.

You see, Washington had bad teeth. That part of the story is fact. He had to wear dentures—false teeth. For centuries, people said that those false teeth were carved from wood. It turns out the *story* was false.

In recent years, scientists got their hands on some sets of Washington's dentures. They **analyzed** the material in the teeth. The scientists found gold. They found ivory from a hippo's teeth. They found cow teeth. They even found human teeth. But they didn't find any wood.

So Washington's dentures may have been weird. But at least they did not give him splinters.

 **ELVIS PRESLEY IS STILL ALIVE.**

Just last year, a famous rock star was seen in a shopping mall. Later, he turned up at a grocery store.

The rock star is Elvis Presley. People see him all over. That is kind of weird. Why? Elvis died on August 16, 1977.

So, what are all the sightings about? Many fans believe Elvis faked his death. They say they have proof. For instance, Elvis's middle name was Aron. On his gravestone, it's misspelled: Aaron. Sounds like a simple mistake. But some people say it means Elvis is alive!

Here is more "proof." Elvis sometimes traveled in disguise. He used a fake name: Jon Burrows. Right after Elvis died, a guy named Jon Burrows left the country. That must have been Elvis, right? Wrong!

Sadly, many people witnessed Elvis dying or dead. He definitely is not alive.

It's always nice to help someone in need. Maybe you will even get a reward. But you probably won't get one this big!

In 2000, a couple went out for a drive. They spotted a driver in trouble. He had a flat tire. He did not know how to change it. So, the couple pulled over and helped.

The driver wanted to reward them. So, he wrote down their names and address. A week later, he sent them $10,000!

Who was that mystery driver? He was Bill Gates, the founder of Microsoft. He is one of the richest people in the world. He is also the subject of a common myth!

The flat-tire story never happened. But similar stories have been told for years. People like to tell stories about the very rich. They especially like to think about getting a share of the wealth!

MYTH | BETSY ROSS SEWED THE FIRST AMERICAN FLAG.

Have you ever heard of Betsy Ross? In 1776, the United States had just become a free country. President George Washington asked Ross to sew the first American flag.

He wanted the flag to have stars with six points. Betsy suggested five-point stars. Washington agreed. The rest is history.

But in this case, history might not be **accurate**. Did Ross really sew the first flag? There is no written record of her meeting with Washington. Also, the very first flag did not have five-point stars. Those stars were not used until 1782.

The Betsy Ross story was first told by her grandson. Back then, the United States was still a new country. People liked the story of the **patriotic** seamstress. But with no record of the meeting, historians say the story is just a myth.

People have some interesting ideas about animals. Not all of those ideas are correct .

CHAPTER

4 | Animal Crackers

MYTH THE COLOR RED MAKES BULLS ANGRY.

How does a bullfighter **provoke** a bull to charge? (And how can you **avoid** such an event?) Many people think the red cape is to blame. They say that red makes bulls mad! After all, bullfighters have used red capes since the 1700s.

It's true that the cape provokes bulls. But its color has nothing to do with it. It's the movement of the cape that makes a bull charge. To keep a bull from attacking you, stay out of its way. At least, stand still!

Bulls do not really get angry when they see red. ▶

29

MYTH DOGS' MOUTHS ARE CLEANER THAN HUMAN MOUTHS.

Do you know any dog owners who let their pets "kiss" them? Do you let your dog slobber on you? Many humans believe that dogs' mouths are cleaner than ours.

How did this myth get started? There are two possible reasons. First, dogs lick their wounds to help the wounds heal. So it seems that a dog's **saliva** has healing powers. Second, dogs usually have healthy teeth. They don't get very many cavities. Their mouths probably have fewer cavity-causing bacteria than humans' do. But that doesn't mean that a dog's mouth is cleaner than a human's.

In truth, a dog's mouth has the same amount of bacteria as a human mouth. It's the type of bacteria that is different.

So, let your dog be your best friend. But think twice about letting him kiss you!

You may want to think twice about letting your dog slobber all over you.

 **BATS ARE BLIND.**

You have probably heard the saying "As blind as a bat!" Now, it's time to shed some light on that saying.

The truth is, most bats are *not* blind. In fact, all healthy bats can see. They use their vision to tell time. When the sun goes down, bats can see that it is dark out. They know it is nighttime. For bats, that means it is time to hunt.

It is true that bats don't use sight to hunt. Instead, they use a **method** called echolocation. As a bat flies, it makes squeaky sounds. When the sounds bounce off a bug, they echo back to the bat. That tells the bat where to find the bug—and gobble it up!

Why do bats use this method? It is not because they are blind. They use echolocation because it's nighttime. Just like us, bats cannot see well in the dark!

MYTH A GROUNDHOG'S SHADOW DETERMINES THE LENGTH OF WINTER.

Groundhog Day happens on February 2 every year. According to legend, the groundhog—a type of rodent—comes out of its underground home on that day.

If the sun is shining, the groundhog sees its shadow and goes back underground. That means we get six more weeks of winter. If the day is cloudy, the groundhog stays outdoors. Spring is on the way!

You probably think that doesn't sound very scientific, and you are right! It is just a myth. It started in Germany in ancient times. People did not know much about the weather, so they used rodents to predict it.

The tradition is amusing, but it is not very accurate. Weather experts say that groundhogs' **predictions** are correct only 40% of the time. You would get similar odds if you flipped a coin.

 **A CENTIPEDE HAS 100 LEGS.**

There are 100 *cent*s in a dollar. There are 100 years in a *cent*ury. There are 100 *cent*imeters in a meter. Do you see a pattern? That's right! The root *cent* means "one hundred."

So, what is the deal with centipedes? You have seen them. They are those creepy, long bugs with many legs. How many? The name *centipede* must mean they have 100 legs! Right?

Well, *centipede* does mean "hundred-legged." But very few centipedes have exactly 100 legs. Believe it or not, some have as many as 200! But most centipedes have only 30 or 42 legs. That's still a lot more than most creatures have!

Maybe the person who named centipedes was guessing. But no matter what you call them, they have a lot of legs!

MYTH CAMELS STORE WATER IN THEIR HUMPS.

Camels rarely get thirsty. Why would they? They carry water in their humps.

Well, that's what many people think, anyway. But those people are wrong. Camels' humps don't hold water. Instead, they hold up to 80 pounds of fat.

That might sound gross. But the fat is a lifesaver. Camels live in the desert. It is hard to find food there. When camels do find food, they fill up. They store extra food as fat, in their humps. Camels use the fat for energy when they must go a long time without food.

So, why do people think camels carry water? Well, camels drink up to 30 gallons of water at once. They can go for six months without drinking. So, water in their humps seems possible. But camels really store water in their stomachs.

MYTH ELEPHANTS ARE AFRAID OF MICE.

Elephants are the largest land animals on Earth. They can weigh up to 15,000 pounds. They can stand as high as 14 feet tall. They are *huge.* So, why would an elephant fear a tiny mouse?

Yet, many people believe that they do. The myth that elephants are afraid of mice goes back to the year 77. That's when a Roman writer said "the elephant hates the mouse" more than any other creature. Many people believed him. Many still do.

The real truth is that elephants have poor eyesight. So, most of the time, they never even see mice. But elephants do hear noises. They sense movements, too. When it can't see where noises and movements are coming from, an elephant thinks it is in danger.

If an elephant hears a mouse, it may

step away. But the elephant would react that way to any creature that it could not see. So, elephants don't need to be braver. But maybe they need eyeglasses!

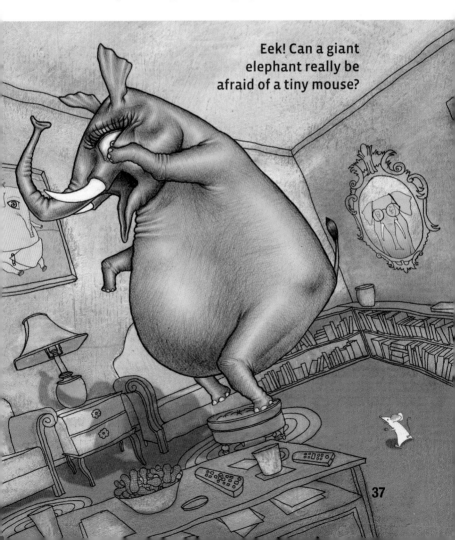

Eek! Can a giant elephant really be afraid of a tiny mouse?

Glossary

accurate *(adjective)* exactly correct

analyzed *(verb)* examined carefully

avoid *(verb)* stay away from

bacteria *(noun)* tiny life forms that live all around you and inside you

data *(noun)* information

digest *(verb)* to break down eaten food so that it can be used by the body

effective *(adjective)* working very well

flammable *(adjective)* burns easily

impact *(noun)* the striking of one thing against another

improve *(verb)* to make better

infamous *(adjective)* known for doing something evil

infected *(adjective)* affected by harmful bacteria or a virus

method *(noun)* way of doing something

mucus *(noun)* a thick fluid that coats and protects your mouth, nose, and throat

nutrients *(noun)* substances needed by people, animals, and plants to stay healthy

offensive *(adjective)* insulting; mean; not sensitive to others' feelings

patriotic *(adjective)* having or showing great love for your country

predictions *(noun)* statements about what you think will happen in the future

provoke *(verb)* upset; make angry

saliva *(noun)* the clear liquid in your mouth

virus *(noun)* a tiny life form that causes diseases

witnessed *(verb)* saw something happen